THE HOME

SLIMMING

THE KITCHEN LIBRARY
SLIMMING

Rhona Newman

HAMLYN

CONTENTS

This edition published in 1991 by
The Hamlyn Publishing Group Limited,
part of Reed International Books,
Michelin House, 81 Fulham Road,
London SW3 6RB.

© Reed International Books Limited 1980

ISBN 0 600 57216 1

Produced by Mandarin Offset
Printed and bound in Hong Kong

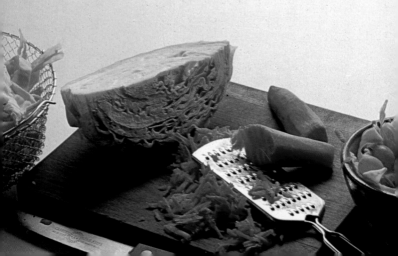

INTRODUCTION

In recent years obesity has become more common among people of all ages. The combination of too many high-calorie foods and not enough exercise is usually blamed for those unwanted pounds and inches. Fortunately the problems that excess weight can cause are now being realised; many people are adopting new, healthier eating patterns and participating in sport to a greater extent.

If you want to lose weight, you must reduce your calorie intake by controlling the amount of food and drink you consume so that your body is receiving less energy than it requires. Only then will the body be forced to draw on its fat reserves.

The recipes in this book are especially designed to form part of a calorie-controlled diet. They provide interesting, tasty dishes, containing generous amounts of protein, vitamins and minerals; reduced amounts of fat and very little carbohydrate. When cooking for a low-calorie diet, it is important to calculate the calories, so use scales for weighing food accurately. Avoid frying for flavour and instead make good use of marinades, fresh herbs and spices. Natural yogurt is an excellent diet food as it can be used instead of cream to enhance flavour.

On reaching a target weight, avoid reverting to old eating habits which will only put the weight back on. Instead follow your new eating plan, adding extra vegetables and wholemeal bread, for example.

NOTES

Standard spoon measurements are used in all recipes
1 tablespoon = one 15 ml spoon   1 teaspoon = one 5 ml spoon
All spoon measures are level.

Fresh herbs are used unless otherwise stated. If unobtainable substitute a bouquet garni of the equivalent dried herbs, or use dried herbs instead but halve the quantities stated.

Use freshly ground black pepper where pepper is specified.

Ovens should be preheated to the specified temperature.

For all recipes, quantities are given in both metric and imperial measures. Follow either set but not a mixture of both, because they are not interchangeable.

Energy values for every recipe are given in calories and the metric equivalent, kilojoules (kJ). These values are approximate.

Tomato and Carrot Soup

1 x 397 g (14 oz)
  can tomatoes,
  chopped
2 large carrots, grated
1 small onion, finely
  chopped
300 ml (½ pint)
  stock
1 teaspoon oregano
grated nutmeg
salt
1 bay leaf
1 teaspoon brown
  sugar
1 tablespoon chopped
  parsley to garnish

Place the tomatoes and their juice in a saucepan. Add the carrot, onion, stock, oregano, nutmeg and salt to taste, bay leaf and sugar. Bring to the boil, stirring, cover and simmer for 30 minutes. Pour into a hot tureen and sprinkle with parsley.

Serves 4
Calories per portion: 40 (167 kJ)

Curry Choux Balls

CHOUX PASTRY:

40 g (1½ oz) low-calorie spread

150 ml (¼ pint) water

50 g (2 oz) plain flour, sifted

2 eggs, beaten

FILLING:

250 g (8 oz) cottage cheese, sieved

4 tablespoons natural low-fat yogurt

curry paste to taste

1 tablespoon chopped parsley

TO GARNISH:

few lettuce leaves

watercress

Place the low-calorie spread and water in a saucepan and heat gently until the fat has melted and the liquid comes to the boil. Remove from the heat and quickly beat in the flour. Continue beating over a low heat until the mixture leaves the sides of the pan. Cool slightly, then beat in the eggs a little at a time.

Spoon the mixture into a piping bag, fitted with a 1 cm (½ inch) plain nozzle, and pipe 15 to 20 small bun shapes on to a greased baking tray. Bake in a preheated hot oven, 220°C (425°F), Gas Mark 7, for 10 minutes, then lower the heat to 180°C (350°F), Gas Mark 4, and cook for a further 15 minutes. Make a slit in the side of each choux ball. Cool on a wire rack.

Mix the filling ingredients in a bowl. Halve the choux balls and spoon in the filling. Serve garnished with lettuce and watercress.

Makes 15 to 20

Calories per choux ball: 30 (126 kJ)

Onion and Watercress Soup

1 bunch watercress
2 onions, sliced
900 ml (1 ½ pints)
    light stock
grated nutmeg
salt and pepper
40 g (1 ½ oz)
    skimmed milk
    powder
few watercress leaves
    to garnish

Wash the watercress, remove the coarse stalks and chop roughly. Place in a pan with the onions, stock and grated nutmeg, salt and pepper to taste. Bring to the boil, cover and simmer for 20 minutes. Leave to cool slightly.

Place the soup in an electric blender with the skimmed milk powder. Blend until smooth then return to the pan. Bring to the boil, stirring, and cook for 1 to 2 minutes. Check the seasoning and pour into hot bowls. Garnish with watercress.

Serves 4
Calories per portion: 50 (209 kJ)

Bortsch

2 teaspoons oil
1 onion, chopped
2 celery sticks,
   chopped
350 g (12 oz)
   beetroot, chopped
125 g (4 oz) white
   cabbage, shredded
900 ml (1 ½ pints)
   stock
1 tablespoon vinegar
salt and pepper
1 bay leaf
3 tablespoons water
   (approximately)
150 g (5 oz) natural
   low-fat yogurt

Heat the oil in a pan, add the onion
and celery and fry until soft. Add the
beetroot and cabbage, then stir in the
stock, vinegar, salt and pepper to
taste, and bay leaf. Bring to the boil,
cover and simmer for 1 hour.

Leave to cool slightly, remove the
bay leaf then purée in an electric
blender or rub through a sieve.
Return to the pan, adding just
enough water to give a pouring
consistency. Check the seasoning and
reheat.

Pour into hot serving bowls and
stir in a little yogurt. Serve
immediately.

Serves 4
Calories per portion: 90 (377 kJ)

French Onion Soup

350 g (12 oz)
  onions, sliced
900 ml (1½ pints)
  beef stock
salt and pepper
2 slices low-calorie
  bread
50 g (2 oz) Edam
  cheese, grated

Place the onions and stock in a pan. Bring to the boil, cover and simmer for 20 minutes. Add salt and pepper to taste.

Toast the bread lightly on both sides and cut into quarters. Pour the soup into individual ovenproof bowls. Top each one with two pieces of bread. Sprinkle with the cheese and place the bowls under a hot grill until the cheese has melted. Serve immediately.

Serves 4
Calories per portion: 75 (314 kJ)

Mushroom Soup

250 g (8 oz) button
  mushrooms,
  chopped
1 onion, chopped
600 ml (1 pint) light
  stock
1/2 teaspoon mixed
  herbs
salt and pepper
25 g (1 oz) skimmed
  milk powder
1 tablespoon chopped
  parsley to garnish

Place the mushrooms, onion, stock, herbs and salt and pepper to taste in a pan. Bring to the boil, cover and simmer for 20 minutes. Leave to cool slightly. Place the soup in an electric blender with the skimmed milk powder. Blend until smooth then return to the pan. Bring to the boil, stirring, and cook for 1 to 2 minutes. Check the seasoning and pour into a hot tureen. Garnish with parsley.

Serves 4
Calories per portion: 45 (188 kJ)

Mushroom Scallops

few lettuce leaves
125 g (4 oz) button
  mushrooms, sliced
125 g (4 oz) shrimps
2 tablespoons low-
  calorie dressing
salt and pepper
chopped parsley to
  garnish

Place the lettuce on 4 scallop shells or small flat plates, arrange the mushrooms on top and scatter over the shrimps.

Just before serving, spoon the dressing over and sprinkle with salt, pepper and chopped parsley.

Serves 4
Calories per portion: 55 (230 kJ)

11

Crunchy Stuffed Pears

2 dessert pears
lemon juice
125 g (4 oz) cottage
  cheese
25 g (1 oz) walnuts,
  chopped
25 g (1 oz) raisins
½ red dessert apple,
  grated
Worcestershire sauce
salt and pepper
lettuce and tomato to
  garnish

Cut the pears in half, remove the core and sprinkle with lemon juice. Place the remaining ingredients in a bowl, adding Worcestershire sauce, salt and pepper to taste; mix well. Pile the mixture into the pear halves, place each one on a lettuce leaf and garnish with lettuce and tomato.
Serves 4
Calories per portion: 110 (460 kJ)

Haddock and Egg Mousse

175 g (6 oz) smoked
  haddock
1 hard-boiled egg,
  chopped
200 ml (⅓ pint)
  natural low-fat
  yogurt
1 teaspoon gelatine
1 tablespoon water
1 teaspoon lemon
  juice
salt and pepper
watercress and egg
  slices to garnish

Poach the haddock in a little water for 6 minutes. Drain, skin and flake the fish. Mix with the egg and yogurt.
  Place the gelatine in a small bowl with the water and lemon juice and heat over a pan of hot water until dissolved. Cool and fold into the fish mixture with salt and pepper to taste. Spoon into 4 ramekin dishes and chill until set. Garnish with watercress and egg.
Serves 4
Calories per portion: 80 (335 kJ)

Cheese and Fruit Cocktail

2 dessert apples
lemon juice
2 celery sticks,
  chopped
50 g (2 oz) Edam
  cheese, diced
125 g (4 oz) grapes,
  halved and seeded
½ lettuce, shredded
grated rind and juice
  of 1 orange
2 tablespoons natural
  low-fat yogurt

Chop the apples, place in a bowl and sprinkle with lemon juice. Add the celery, cheese and grapes and mix together. Place a little shredded lettuce in the base of 4 dishes. Pile the cheese and fruit mixture on top.
  Mix the orange rind, juice and yogurt together, then pour a little over each cocktail. Serve chilled.
Serves 4
Calories per portion: 90 (377 kJ)

Minted Pears

125 g (4 oz) cottage
  cheese
1 tablespoon freshly
  chopped mint
salt and pepper
1 x 411 g (14½ oz)
  can pear halves,
  drained
few lettuce leaves
few mint sprigs to
  garnish

Mix the cottage cheese with the
chopped mint and salt and pepper to
taste. Divide the mixture between
the pear halves. Arrange the lettuce
on a serving plate and place the pears
on top. Garnish with mint.
Serves 4
Calories per portion: 65 (272 kJ)

14

Piquant Dip

250 g (8 oz) cottage
cheese, sieved
150 g (5 oz) natural
low-fat yogurt
½ red pepper, cored,
seeded and chopped
½ green pepper,
cored, seeded and
chopped
1 tablespoon chopped
cucumber
50 g (2 oz) ham,
chopped
¼ teaspoon made
mustard
dash of Tabasco
sauce
salt and pepper
TO SERVE:
few carrots, cut into
strips
few celery sticks, cut
into strips
1 small cauliflower,
broken into florets

Place the cottage cheese in a bowl
and beat in the yogurt. Add the
remaining ingredients with salt and
pepper to taste; mix well. Pile into a
serving bowl and chill until required.
Serve with the raw vegetables.
Serves 6
Calories per portion: 75 (314 kJ)

Quick Sardine Pâté

1 x 120 g (4¼ oz)
can sardines in oil,
drained
grated rind and juice
of ½ lemon
5 tablespoons natural
low-fat yogurt
50 g (2 oz) cottage
cheese, sieved
2.5 cm (1 inch) piece
cucumber, finely
chopped
garlic salt
freshly ground black
pepper
TO GARNISH:
4 cucumber twists
4 parsley sprigs

Place the sardines in a bowl with the
lemon rind and juice and mash with
a fork until smooth. Beat in the
yogurt, cottage cheese and
cucumber. Season to taste with garlic
salt and black pepper. Place in 4
dishes and chill.
    Garnish with the cucumber and
parsley and serve with crispbreads.
Serves 4
Calories per portion: 80 (335 kJ)

Leeks à la Grecque

350 g (12 oz) leeks
juice of ½ lemon
1 tablespoon oil
1 tablespoon water
1 clove garlic,
    crushed
3 tomatoes, skinned
    and chopped
salt and pepper
chopped parsley to
    garnish

Remove the outer leaves from the leeks and cut into 2.5 cm (1 inch) lengths. Wash thoroughly. Place in a pan with the remaining ingredients, adding salt and pepper to taste.

Heat gently to simmering point, then simmer for 20 minutes. Leave to cool in the liquid, then place in a serving dish and garnish with parsley.

Serves 4
Calories per portion: 70 (293 kJ)

Tangy Grapefruit

2 large grapefruit,
   halved
1/2 green pepper,
   cored, seeded and
   chopped
1 carrot, grated
2.5 cm (1 inch) piece
   of cucumber, diced
freshly ground black
   pepper

Loosen the grapefruit from the skin
and remove, leaving the empty half
grapefruit shells intact. Scallop the
edges of the shells if wished.

Remove the pith from the fruit,
then chop and place in a bowl with
the juice. Add the remaining
ingredients, with pepper to taste, and
mix well. Place in the refrigerator
until required.

Just before serving, pile the
mixture into the grapefruit shells.
Serves 4
Calories per portion: 25 (105 kJ)

17

FISH

Baked Cod Medley

4 cod cutlets
2 teaspoons lemon
   juice
freshly ground black
   pepper
15 g (½ oz) butter
1 onion, finely
   chopped
1 green pepper,
   cored, seeded and
   chopped
3 celery sticks,
   chopped
6 tomatoes, skinned
   and chopped
garlic salt
½ teaspoon oregano
parsley sprigs to
   garnish

Wash and dry the cutlets and place in a shallow, ovenproof dish. Sprinkle with the lemon juice and pepper to taste.

Melt the butter in a pan and lightly fry the onion, green pepper and celery. Add the tomatoes, garlic salt to taste, and oregano. Bring to the boil, cover and simmer for 10 to 15 minutes.

Spoon the vegetables over the fish, cover with foil and cook in a preheated moderate oven 180°C (350°F), Gas Mark 4, for 30 minutes. Serve garnished with parsley.

Serves 4
Calories per portion: 135 (565 kJ)

Mediterranean Salad Platter

250 g (8 oz) cod
 fillet
150 ml (¼ pint)
 water
salt
2 tablespoons low-
 calorie dressing
2 teaspoons lemon
 juice
1 x 198 g (7 oz) can
 tuna steak, drained
 and flaked
2 hard-boiled eggs,
 quartered
freshly ground black
 pepper
1 lettuce, washed and
 drained
4 tomatoes, sliced
TO GARNISH:
1 green pepper,
 cored, seeded and
 cut into rings
6 black olives

Place the cod in a pan, add the water
and salt to taste, then poach for
about 8 minutes until the fish is
tender. Drain, then skin and flake the
fish.

Place the dressing and lemon juice
in a bowl and add the cod, tuna and
eggs. Toss lightly and season to taste
with salt and pepper.

Arrange the outside lettuce leaves
on a large serving plate. Shred the
inside lettuce leaves and place in the
centre of the dish. Pile the fish and
egg mixture on top and arrange the
tomato slices around the sides.
Garnish the top of the fish with
green pepper and black olives.

Serves 4
Calories per portion: 265 (1109 kJ)

Fish Curry

25 g (1 oz)
  margarine
1 onion, chopped
½ green pepper,
  cored, seeded and
  chopped
1 carrot, thinly sliced
3 teaspoons curry
  powder
1 tablespoon plain
  flour
300 ml (½ pint)
  stock
1 teaspoon lemon
  juice
1 small apple,
  peeled, cored and
  chopped
1 tablespoon sultanas
500 g (1 lb) haddock
  fillets, cut into
  cubes
salt and pepper
chopped parsley to
  garnish

Melt the margarine in a pan and fry
the onion, pepper, carrot and curry
powder for 5 minutes. Stir in the
flour and cook for 1 minute.
Gradually blend in the stock and
lemon juice. Heat, stirring until the
sauce thickens.

Add the apple, sultanas and
haddock, then season to taste with
salt and pepper. Cover and simmer
for 20 to 25 minutes.

Transfer to a hot serving dish and
garnish with chopped parsley. Serve
with a selection of accompaniments:
a small portion of boiled rice, sliced
tomato, diced cucumber and natural
low-fat yogurt.

Serves 4
**Calories per portion: 185 (774 kJ)
without accompaniments**

Haddock and Spinach Layer

500 g (1 lb) haddock
  fillets
150 ml (¼ pint)
  skimmed milk
1 bay leaf
salt and pepper
1 hard-boiled egg,
  chopped
500 g (1 lb) frozen
  leaf spinach
SAUCE:
150 ml (¼ pint)
  skimmed milk
  (approximately)
25 g (1 oz)
  margarine
1 onion, chopped
25 g (1 oz) plain
  flour
grated nutmeg
TOPPING:
2 crispbreads, crushed
1 tomato, sliced, to
  garnish

Place the haddock in a pan. Add the milk, bay leaf, salt and pepper to taste, then poach for about 10 minutes until the fish is tender. Drain, reserving the liquor. Flake the haddock and mix with the egg.

Cook the spinach as directed on the packet and drain well.

Make the fish liquor up to 300 ml (½ pint) with extra milk. Melt the margarine in a pan and fry the onion until soft. Stir in the flour and cook for 1 minute. Gradually blend in the milk then bring to the boil, stirring continuously. Cook, stirring, for a further 1 minute. Season to taste with salt, pepper and nutmeg. Stir in the fish and egg mixture; mix well.

Layer the spinach and fish mixture in a greased 1.2 litre (2 pint) ovenproof dish, finishing with a layer of spinach. Sprinkle with the crispbreads and cook in a preheated moderate oven, 180°C (350°F), Gas Mark 4, for 20 to 30 minutes.

Garnish with tomato slices.

Serves 4
Calories per portion: 220 (921 kJ)

Orange and Pepper Stuffed Plaice

4 plaice fillets
salt and pepper
STUFFING:
1 green pepper,
  cored, seeded and
  chopped
50 g (2 oz)
  low-calorie
  breadcrumbs
grated rind and juice
  of 1 orange
TO GARNISH:
green pepper rings
orange slices

Skin the plaice fillets and sprinkle with salt and pepper. Place on a flat surface.

Mix together the green pepper, breadcrumbs and half the orange rind. Add salt and pepper to taste and bind with a little orange juice. Divide the stuffing between the fillets, roll up and secure with cocktail sticks.

Place in a shallow ovenproof dish and sprinkle with the remaining orange rind, salt and pepper. Pour the remaining orange juice over the fish and cook in a preheated moderate oven, 180°C (350°F), Gas Mark 4, for 30 minutes or until the fish is tender. Remove the cocktail sticks.

Serve garnished with green pepper rings and orange slices.
Serves 4
Calories per portion: 130 (544 kJ)

Herrings with Apple and Horseradish

4 small herrings,
  filleted
salt and pepper
2 tablespoons
  horseradish sauce
2 dessert apples,
  cored and grated
2 tablespoons cider
2-3 drops liquid
  sweetener
watercress to garnish

Place the herrings in a pan and add just enough water to cover. Add salt and pepper to taste. Bring to the boil, then lower the heat, cover and simmer for 10 to 15 minutes. Remove from the pan, drain well and keep hot.

Place the horseradish sauce in a pan with the apples and cider. Bring to the boil, then simmer for 3 minutes. Add sweetener to taste.

Arrange the fish on a warmed serving plate and top with the sauce. Garnish with watercress.
Serves 4
Calories per portion: 250 (1047 kJ)

Mackerel with Mustard and Oats

4 x 175 g (6 oz)
    mackerel fillets
2 teaspoons lemon
    juice
salt and pepper
25 g (1 oz) porridge
    oats
2 teaspoons made
    mustard
TO GARNISH:
parsley sprigs
lemon twists

Place the mackerel on a grill rack
lined with foil. Sprinkle with lemon
juice and salt and pepper to taste.

Mix the oats and mustard together
and spread lightly over the mackerel.
Cook under a medium grill for 10 to
15 minutes. Transfer to a hot serving
dish and garnish with parsley and
lemon twists.

Serves 4
Calories per portion: 335 (1402 kJ)

Kedgeree

500 g (1 lb) smoked
  haddock
200 ml (⅓ pint)
  skimmed milk
150 g (5 oz)
  long-grain rice
1 hard-boiled egg,
  chopped
125 g (4 oz) peas,
  cooked
salt and pepper
parsley sprig to
  garnish

Poach the haddock in the milk for 10
minutes or until tender; drain,
reserving the liquor. Flake the fish
and remove any skin.

Cook the rice in plenty of boiling
salted water until tender. Drain and
rinse thoroughly, then return to the
pan.

Stir in the fish, egg, peas and a
little of the fish liquor. Season with
salt and pepper to taste, then place
over a low heat until heated through.
Transfer to a warmed serving dish
and garnish with parsley.

Serves 4
Calories per portion: 275 (1151 kJ)

Cheddar Cod

4 cod cutlets or steaks
2 teaspoons lemon
   juice
salt and pepper
SAUCE:
25 g (1 oz)
   margarine
25 g (1 oz) plain
   flour
300 ml (½ pint)
   skimmed milk
75 g (3 oz) Cheddar
   cheese, grated
½ teaspoon made
   mustard
TO GARNISH:
parsley sprigs
1 tomato, cut into
   quarters

Wash and dry the cod and place in a shallow ovenproof dish. Sprinkle with the lemon juice and salt and pepper to taste.

Place the margarine, flour and milk in a pan. Heat, whisking continuously until the sauce thickens. Continue cooking for 1 minute. Stir in the cheese, mustard and salt and pepper to taste.

Pour the sauce over the cod and cook in a preheated moderate oven, 180°C (350°F), Gas Mark 4, for 30 minutes. Garnish with parsley and tomato wedges.
Serves 4
Calories per portion: 245 (1026 kJ)

Turbot and Prawn Creole

1 onion, chopped
1 green pepper,
    cored, seeded and
    chopped
1 x 397 g (14 oz)
    can tomatoes
½ teaspoon basil
½ teaspoon oregano
pinch of sugar
salt and pepper
250 g (8 oz) turbot
    (or other white
    fish), cut into
    cubes
250 g (8 oz) peeled
    prawns
2 teaspoons cornflour
2 tablespoons dry
    white wine
TO GARNISH:
whole prawns
chopped parsley

Place the onion, green pepper, tomatoes and their juice, basil, oregano and sugar in a pan. Add salt and pepper to taste. Bring to the boil, cover and simmer for 15 minutes.

Add the turbot and peeled prawns and simmer for a further 10 to 15 minutes. Blend the cornflour and wine until smooth, then stir into the sauce. Heat until the sauce thickens and continue cooking for 2 minutes.

Transfer to a hot serving dish and garnish with whole prawns and chopped parsley.

Serves 4
Calories per portion: 160 (670 kJ)

Smoked Haddock with Vegetables

1 onion, finely
    chopped
1 celery stick, finely
    chopped
1 carrot, grated
2 tablespoons frozen
    peas
salt and pepper
500 g (1 lb) smoked
    haddock fillet
15 g (½ oz) butter
6 tablespoons tomato
    juice
parsley sprigs to
    garnish

Place the onion, celery, carrot and peas in a shallow ovenproof dish. Sprinkle with salt and pepper.

Cut the haddock into 4 portions and arrange on top of the vegetables. Dot with the butter and spoon the tomato juice over the fish. Cover with foil and cook in a preheated moderately hot oven, 190°C (375°F), Gas Mark 5, for 30 minutes. Serve garnished with parsley.

Serves 4
Calories per portion: 180 (753 kJ)

POULTRY & MEAT

Italian Chicken

4 chicken breasts,
   skinned and boned
50 g (2 oz) lean
   ham, cut into 4
   pieces
150 ml (¼ pint)
   chicken stock
1 tablespoon sherry
1 red pepper, cored,
   seeded and sliced
STUFFING:
40 g (1½ oz)
   low-calorie
   breadcrumbs
50 g (2 oz)
   Parmesan cheese,
   grated
1 small onion, finely
   chopped
2 teaspoons chopped
   parsley
1 tablespoon sherry
salt and pepper
TO GARNISH:
watercress sprigs

Mix together the stuffing
ingredients, with salt and pepper to
taste, and press to the underside of
the chicken breasts. Place a piece of
ham over the top. Arrange the
chicken in a casserole, pour over the
stock and sherry and add the red
pepper.

   Cover and cook in a preheated
moderate oven, 180°C (350°F), Gas
Mark 4, for 1 hour or until the
chicken is cooked, basting
occasionally with the liquid. Garnish
with watercress.

Serves 4
Calories per portion: 270 (1130 kJ)

Chicken in Lemon Sauce

4 chicken joints,
  skinned
grated rind and juice
  of 1 lemon
1 small onion,
  chopped
1 celery stick,
  chopped
few thyme sprigs
salt and pepper
300 ml (½ pint)
  chicken stock
25 g (1 oz)
  margarine
25 g (1 oz) plain
  flour
TO GARNISH:
watercress
lemon twists

Place the chicken in a 1.75 litre (3 pint) casserole. Add the lemon rind and juice, onion, celery, thyme, salt and pepper to taste, and the stock. Cover and cook in a preheated moderately hot oven, 190°C (375°F), Gas Mark 5, for 1 hour or until the chicken is tender.

Transfer the chicken to a serving dish and keep hot. Strain the stock.

Melt the margarine in a pan and stir in the flour. Cook for 1 minute, then remove from the heat and gradually blend in the stock from the chicken. Return to the heat and cook, stirring, until thickened. Check the seasoning and pour over the chicken. Garnish with watercress and lemon.

Serves 4
Calories per portion: 240 (1005 kJ)

Chicken in Sweet and Sour Sauce

4 chicken joints,
    skinned
1 green pepper, cored,
    seeded and chopped
1 red pepper, cored,
    seeded and chopped
1 onion, sliced
1 x 227 g (8 oz) can
    pineapple pieces,
    drained
1 tablespoon soy
    sauce
1 tablespoon vinegar
1 x 227 g (8 oz) can
    tomatoes
150 ml (¼ pint)
    water
salt
½ teaspoon sugar

Place the chicken in a 1.75 litre (3 pint) casserole and cook, uncovered, in a preheated moderately hot oven, 190°C (375°F), Gas Mark 5, for 15 minutes.

Place the remaining ingredients, with salt to taste, in a pan. Bring to the boil, stirring, cover and simmer for 20 minutes. Pour the sauce over the chicken and return to the oven for a further 30 minutes or until the chicken is tender, basting occasionally with the sauce. Serve with green vegetables.

Serves 4
Calories per portion: 210 (879 kJ)

Turkey Sicilian Style

25 g (1 oz) butter
1 onion, sliced
75 g (3 oz) button
  mushrooms, sliced
25 g (1 oz) plain
  flour
½ teaspoon ground
  ginger
½ teaspoon grated
  nutmeg
150 ml (¼ pint)
  chicken stock
150 ml (¼ pint)
  skimmed milk
350 g (12 oz) cooked
  turkey meat,
  chopped
salt and pepper
15 g (½ oz) flaked
  almonds, toasted

Melt the butter in a large pan, add
the onion and mushrooms and fry
for 5 minutes or until soft. Add the
flour, ginger and nutmeg. Cook for
1 minute. Gradually blend in the
stock and milk. Bring to the boil,
stirring, then add the turkey and salt
and pepper to taste. Cover and
simmer for 20 minutes.

Pile the mixture into a hot serving
dish and sprinkle with the toasted
almonds. Serve with a small portion
of noodles and salad.
Serves 4
Calories per portion: 275 (1151 kJ)

Chicken with Aubergines and Courgettes

1 aubergine, sliced
1 teaspoon salt
1 x 1.5 kg (3 lb) chicken
1 onion, sliced
2 cloves garlic, crushed
3 courgettes, sliced
4 tomatoes, skinned and chopped
2 tablespoons tomato purée
300 ml (½ pint) chicken stock
1½ teaspoons cumin seeds
salt and pepper
½ teaspoon sugar
chopped parsley to garnish

Place the aubergine slices on a plate and sprinkle with the salt. Leave for 1 hour then rinse and drain.

Divide the chicken into 8 pieces and remove the skin. Place in a 1.75 litre (3 pint) casserole and cook, uncovered, in a preheated moderately hot oven, 190°C (375°F), Gas Mark 5, for 30 minutes.

Place the aubergine slices in a pan with the remaining ingredients, seasoning to taste with salt and pepper. Bring to the boil, cover and simmer for 10 minutes. Pour into the casserole and return to the oven for 40 to 50 minutes. Serve garnished with chopped parsley.

Serves 4
Calories per portion: 190 (795 kJ)

Paprika Lamb

4 lamb chops
1 onion, finely
   chopped
150 g (5 oz) natural
   low-fat yogurt
2 teaspoons paprika
MARINADE:
2 tablespoons white
   wine
2 teaspoons lemon
   juice
½ teaspoon sugar
½ teaspoon dried
   thyme
salt and pepper
TO GARNISH:
paprika
parsley sprigs

Mix together the marinade
ingredients, with salt and pepper to
taste. Trim the chops and remove
any excess fat. Place in the marinade
and leave for 2 to 3 hours.

Drain the chops and dry with
kitchen paper. Place them in a
shallow ovenproof dish. Sprinkle the
onion over the chops and cover with
foil. Cook in a preheated moderately
hot oven, 190°C (375°F), Gas Mark
5, for 1 hour.

Mix the yogurt with the paprika
and spoon over the chops. Continue
cooking for a further 15 minutes.
Serve sprinkled with paprika and
garnished with parsley.
Serves 4
Calories per portion: 240 (1005 kJ)

Liver with Orange and Thyme

1 tablespoon olive oil
500 g (1 lb) lambs'
liver, sliced
1 green pepper,
cored, seeded and
cut into rings
grated rind and juice
of 2 oranges
1 chicken stock cube
1 teaspoon dried
thyme
salt and pepper
orange twists to
garnish

Heat the olive oil in a large frying pan, add the liver and cook until brown on both sides. Add the green pepper and orange rind and cook for 2 minutes.

Make the orange juice up to 150 ml (¼ pint) with water and add to the pan. Stir in the crumbled stock cube, thyme and salt and pepper to taste. Bring to the boil and simmer for 15 minutes. Transfer to a hot serving dish and garnish with orange twists.

Serves 4
Calories per portion: 240 (1005 kJ)

Kidney and Ham Provençal

salt and pepper
15 g (½ oz) plain
flour
8 lambs' kidneys,
skinned, cored and
halved
1 onion, sliced
½ green pepper,
cored, seeded and
chopped
50 g (2 oz) button
mushrooms, sliced
1 clove garlic,
crushed
1 x 227 g (8 oz) can
tomatoes
1 teaspoon oregano
150 ml (¼ pint)
stock
1 bay leaf
2 drops liquid
sweetener
50 g (2 oz) lean
ham, cut into
strips
chopped parsley to
garnish

Season the flour with salt and pepper and use to coat the kidneys. Place in a pan with the onion, green pepper, mushrooms, garlic, tomatoes and their juice, oregano, salt and pepper to taste, stock and bay leaf. Bring to the boil, cover and simmer for 25 to 30 minutes.

Add the sweetener and the ham and continue cooking for 5 minutes. Transfer to a hot serving dish and garnish with chopped parsley.

Serves 4
Calories per portion: 180 (753 kJ)

Middle Eastern Lamb Chops

4 lamb chops
1 x 212 g (7½ oz)
    can mandarin
    oranges, drained
SAUCE:
300 ml (½ pint)
    stock
150 g (5 oz) natural
    low-fat yogurt
1 tablespoon tomato
    purée
2 tablespoons
    chutney
1 tablespoon curry
    powder
1 tablespoon
    desiccated coconut
1 onion, chopped
1 apple, peeled,
    cored and
    quartered
salt and pepper
watercress to garnish

Trim the chops and remove any
excess fat. Place in a 1.2 litre (2 pint)
casserole. Reserve a few mandarins
for garnish, and place the remainder
over the chops.

Place the sauce ingredients, with
salt and pepper to taste, in an electric
blender and work to a purée. Pour
the sauce over the chops, cover and
cook in a preheated moderate oven,
180°C (350°F), Gas Mark 4, for 1¼
hours or until the meat is tender.

As the sauce separates a little
during cooking, transfer the chops to
a hot serving dish, stir the sauce and
spoon over the chops. Garnish with
the remaining oranges and
watercress.
Serves 4
Calories per portion: 330 (1381 kJ)

Dolmades

125 g (4 oz)
    long-grain rice
1 onion, finely
    chopped
1 clove garlic,
    crushed
2 tomatoes, skinned
    and chopped
600 ml (1 pint) light
    stock
250 g (8 oz) cooked
    lamb, minced
½ teaspoon
    powdered
    rosemary
salt and pepper
12-16 fresh vine or
    cabbage leaves
juice of ½ lemon
15 g (½ oz) butter
150 g (5 oz) natural
    low-fat yogurt to
    serve (optional)

Pour boiling water over the rice and drain. Place in a pan with the onion, garlic and tomatoes. Add enough stock to cover the rice then bring to the boil. Simmer gently until the rice is cooked, adding water if the mixture becomes too dry.

Leave the rice to cool then stir in the minced lamb, rosemary and salt and pepper to taste.

Blanch the vine or cabbage leaves in boiling salted water for 4 minutes. Drain and remove the coarse stalks. Place the leaves on a flat surface and divide the rice and meat mixture between them. Fold the leaves, enclosing the filling, to make small neat parcels. Pack them closely in layers in a flameproof casserole.

Add the remaining stock and the lemon juice. Dot with butter and place a plate inside the casserole to keep the parcels under the liquid. Cover and simmer for 45 minutes.

Remove the parcels with a perforated spoon and arrange on a warm serving dish. Serve the yogurt in a separate dish if used.

Serves 4
Calories per portion: 290 (1214 kJ)
without yogurt

Mushroom Stuffed Breast of Lamb

750 g (1 ½ lb) boned
  breast of lamb
STUFFING:
125 g (4 oz)
  mushrooms, finely
  chopped
125 g (4 oz) cottage
  cheese
1 teaspoon powdered
  rosemary
1 celery stick,
  chopped
finely grated rind of
  1 lemon
salt and pepper

Trim away any excess fat from the lamb. Mix together the stuffing ingredients, with salt and pepper to taste.

Place the lamb on a flat surface and spread the stuffing over, to within 1 cm (½ inch) of the edges. Roll up and secure with string and meat skewers.

Place on a rack in a roasting pan and cover with foil. Cook in a preheated cool oven, 150°C (300°F), Gas Mark 2, for 3 hours.

Remove the string and skewers and place the meat on a hot serving dish. Serve with a selection of cooked vegetables.

Serves 4
Calories per portion: 375 (1570 kJ)

Liver and Sausage Barbecue Casserole

125 g (4 oz) beef
  chipolatas
350 g (12 oz) lambs'
  liver, sliced
1 onion, sliced
1 x 283 g (10 oz)
  can tomato soup
2 teaspoons Worcester-
  shire sauce
1 teaspoon vinegar
1 teaspoon made
  mustard
salt and pepper
chopped parsley to
  garnish

Grill the sausages on a rack until just cooked. Cool and cut into pieces.

Place the liver in a 1.2 litre (2 pint) casserole with the sausages and onion. Blend the soup with the Worcestershire sauce, vinegar and mustard. Season to taste with salt and pepper and pour into the casserole. Cover and cook in a preheated moderate oven, 180°C (350°F), Gas Mark 4, for 1 hour or until the liver is tender. Garnish with chopped parsley.

Serves 4
Calories per portion: 285 (1193 kJ)

Pork Curry

1 tablespoon oil
2 cloves, crushed
½ teaspoon ground
  ginger
1 ½ teaspoons ground
  coriander
1 teaspoon ground
  turmeric
1 teaspoon cumin seeds
½ teaspoon ground
  cinnamon
½ teaspoon ground
  fenugreek
½ teaspoon chilli
  powder
250 g (8 oz) onions,
  sliced
4 cloves garlic, crushed
350 g (12 oz)
  tomatoes, skinned
  and chopped
150 ml (¼ pint) stock
salt and pepper
15 g (½ oz) flour
500 g (1 lb) pork
  fillet, cut into
  cubes

Heat the oil in a pan and add the cloves, ginger, coriander, turmeric, cumin, cinnamon, fenugreek and chilli. Fry the spices for 2 minutes then add the onions and garlic. Cook for 1 minute then add the tomatoes, stock and salt to taste.

Season the flour with salt and pepper and use to coat the pork. Add to the curry sauce, bring to the boil, cover and simmer for 1½ hours or until the meat is cooked and the sauce is reduced to a thick gravy. Transfer to a hot serving dish. Serve with a selection of accompaniments: a small portion of boiled rice, sliced cucumber, sliced tomatoes, sliced banana in lemon juice and natural low-fat yogurt.

Serves 4
Calories per portion: 380 (1591 kJ) without accompaniments

Meatballs in Tomato Sauce

MEATBALLS:
500 g (1 lb) lean
   minced beef
1 clove garlic,
   crushed
1 tablespoon chopped
   parsley
½ teaspoon cumin
   seeds (optional)
salt and pepper
1 egg, beaten
SAUCE:
2 onions, finely
   chopped
1 x 397 g (14 oz)
   can tomatoes
1 tablespoon tomato
   purée
½ teaspoon sugar
grated nutmeg
TO GARNISH:
chopped parsley

Put the beef, garlic, parsley, cumin seeds (if using) and salt and pepper to taste in a bowl; mix well. Bind the mixture with the egg, then divide into 20 and shape into balls on a floured surface.

Place the sauce ingredients, with nutmeg, salt and pepper to taste, in a large flameproof casserole. Bring to the boil, then lower the heat. Carefully place the meatballs in the liquid, cover and simmer gently for 40 to 45 minutes, stirring occasionally.

Transfer the meatballs to a hot serving dish and pour the sauce over. Serve garnished with chopped parsley.
Serves 4
Calories per portion: 330 (1381 kJ)

Frankfurters and Cabbage

500 g (1 lb) red
   cabbage, shredded
1 onion, chopped
1 cooking apple,
   peeled, cored and
   chopped
1 clove garlic, crushed
1 tablespoon vinegar
15 g (½ oz)
   margarine
1 teaspoon brown
   sugar
1 teaspoon caraway
   seeds
salt and pepper
3 tablespoons water
12 frankfurters,
   cooked and kept
   hot
chopped parsley to
   garnish

Put the cabbage, onion, apple, garlic, vinegar, margarine, sugar, caraway seeds and salt and pepper to taste in a large saucepan. Place over a low heat, cover and cook for 5 minutes, shaking the pan occasionally.

Add the water, bring to the boil and simmer for 40 minutes. Arrange the cabbage on a hot serving dish. Pile the hot frankfurters into the centre and sprinkle with chopped parsley.
Serves 4
Calories per portion: 300 (1256 kJ)

Kebabs

125 g (4 oz)
  gammon steak, cut
  into 2.5 cm
  (1 inch) pieces
4 lambs' kidneys,
  halved
125 g (4 oz) lambs'
  liver, cut into 2.5
  cm (1 inch) cubes
4 beef chipolatas,
  twisted in the
  centre and halved
2 tomatoes, quartered
50 g (2 oz) button
  mushrooms
1 green pepper,
  cored, seeded and
  cut into 2.5 cm
  (1 inch) squares
1 onion, cut into
  pieces
1 tablespoon oil
SAUCE:
150 g (5 oz) natural
  low-fat yogurt
1 teaspoon made
  mustard
2 teaspoons tomato
  ketchup
2 teaspoons
  Worcestershire
  sauce
salt and pepper
TO SERVE:
500 g (1 lb) white
  cabbage, shredded
1 teaspoon caraway
  seeds

Thread the first 8 ingredients onto 4 skewers and brush lightly with the oil. Cook under a preheated moderate grill for 20 minutes, turning occasionally.

Combine the sauce ingredients with salt and pepper to taste; mix thoroughly.

Cook the cabbage in boiling salted water for 5 minutes, add the caraway seeds and cook for a further 1 minute. Drain the cabbage and arrange on a warm serving dish. Place the kebabs on top and serve the sauce separately.

Serves 4
Calories per portion: 300 (1256 kJ)
Sauce: 20 (84 kJ)

Ham with Pineapple and Yogurt

4 x 75 g (3 oz) ham
   steaks
4 pineapple rings
150 g (5 oz) natural
   low-fat yogurt
1/2 teaspoon made
   mustard
1/2 teaspoon yeast
   extract
salt and pepper
2 tablespoons
   chopped parsley
parsley sprigs to
   garnish

Place the ham steaks in a shallow ovenproof dish and top each one with a pineapple ring. Mix together the yogurt, mustard, yeast extract and salt and pepper to taste. Stir in the chopped parsley and spoon over the ham and pineapple. Cook in a preheated moderate oven, 160°C (325°F), Gas Mark 3, for 30 minutes.

Garnish with parsley sprigs and serve with baked tomatoes if liked.

Serves 4
Calories per portion: 220 (921 kJ)

Flemish Beef

500 g (1 lb) chuck
  steak, cubed
1 onion, sliced
1 carrot, sliced
1 clove garlic, crushed
75 g (3 oz)
  mushrooms, sliced
300 ml (½ pint)
  light ale
1 beef stock cube
1 teaspoon vinegar
1 teaspoon brown
  sugar
grated nutmeg
salt and pepper
1 bay leaf
2 teaspoons cornflour
3 tablespoons water
chopped parsley to
  garnish

Brown the steak in a non-stick frying pan and place in a 1.75 litre (3 pint) casserole. Add the onion, carrot, garlic and mushrooms.

Blend the light ale with the stock cube, vinegar, brown sugar, and nutmeg, salt and pepper to taste. Pour over the meat and vegetables. Add the bay leaf. Cover and cook in a preheated moderate oven, 180°C (350°F), Gas Mark 4, for 1½ hours or until the meat is tender.

Mix the cornflour with the water and stir into the casserole. Cook for 15 to 20 minutes. Serve garnished with chopped parsley.

Serves 4
Calories per portion: 275 (1151 kJ)

Hamburgers with Topping

HAMBURGERS:
350 g (12 oz) lean
  minced beef
1 onion, chopped
15 g (½ oz) low-
  calorie breadcrumbs
1 beef stock cube
1 teaspoon mixed
  herbs
salt and pepper
1 egg, beaten
1 tablespoon oil
TOPPING:
50 g (2 oz)
  mushrooms, chopped
2 teaspoons
  horseradish sauce
25 g (1 oz) Edam
  cheese, grated
TO GARNISH:
few lettuce leaves
1 tomato, quartered
parsley sprigs

Put the beef, onion, breadcrumbs, stock cube, herbs and salt and pepper to taste in a bowl; mix well. Bind the mixture with the egg, then divide into 4 and shape into flat cakes.

Heat the oil in a frying pan and cook the hamburgers for 4 to 5 minutes on each side. Remove from the pan, drain on kitchen paper and keep hot.

To make the topping: add the mushrooms to the pan and fry for 1 minute. Stir in the horseradish and salt and pepper to taste. Spoon over each hamburger and sprinkle with the grated cheese.

Place under a preheated moderate grill until the cheese has melted. Arrange the hamburgers on a warmed serving plate and garnish with lettuce, tomatoes and parsley.

Serves 4
Calories per portion: 290 (1214 kJ)

Soufflé Topped Beef

350 g (12 oz) lean
    minced beef
1 onion, chopped
50 g (2 oz)
    mushrooms,
    chopped
1 carrot, grated
15 g (½ oz) plain
    flour
300 ml (½ pint) beef
    stock
2 teaspoons
    Worcestershire
    sauce
salt and pepper
TOPPING:
2 eggs, separated
125 g (4 oz) frozen
    mixed vegetables,
    cooked

Fry the beef in a pan until brown and
drain off the excess fat. Add the
onion, mushrooms and carrot and
cook for 5 minutes. Add the flour
and cook for 1 minute. Stir in the
stock, Worcestershire sauce and salt
and pepper to taste. Bring to the
boil, cover and simmer for 45
minutes. Transfer to a greased
1.2 litre (2 pint) ovenproof dish.

To make the topping: beat the egg
yolks with a little salt and pepper.
Whisk the egg whites until stiff, then
fold into the yolks. Stir in the mixed
vegetables and spoon over the meat.
Cook in a preheated moderate oven,
180°C (350°F), Gas Mark 4, for 15 to
20 minutes. Serve immediately.

Serves 4
Calories per portion: 225 (1067 kJ)

Hungarian Veal

15 g (½ oz)
  margarine
500 g (1 lb) lean
  veal, cut into cubes
1 onion, sliced
3 teaspoons paprika
1 green pepper,
  cored, seeded and
  chopped
50 g (2 oz) button
  mushrooms, sliced
300 ml (½ pint)
  tomato juice
90 ml (3 fl oz) beef
  stock
½ teaspoon sugar
salt and pepper
grated nutmeg
1 bay leaf
4 tablespoons natural
  low-fat yogurt
chopped parsley to
  garnish

Melt the margarine in a large pan, add the veal and fry for 5 minutes. Add the onion and fry for 2 to 3 minutes. Stir in the paprika and cook for 1 minute. Add the green pepper, mushrooms, tomato juice, stock, sugar, salt, pepper and nutmeg to taste, and the bay leaf. Bring to the boil, stirring, then transfer to a 1.75 litre (3 pint) casserole. Cook in a preheated moderate oven, 180°C (350°F), Gas Mark 4, for 1 to 1½ hours. Stir in the yogurt just before serving. Garnish with chopped parsley.

Serves 4
Calories per portion: 225 (942 kJ)

EGG & CHEESE DISHES

Egg Mornay with Shrimps and Corn

8 hard-boiled eggs,
  halved
50 g (2 oz)
  sweetcorn
1 x 198 g (7 oz) can
  shrimps, drained
1 tablespoon
  cornflour
300 ml (½ pint)
  skimmed milk
¼ teaspoon cayenne
  pepper
salt and pepper
50 g (2 oz) Edam
  cheese, grated
TO GARNISH:
paprika
chopped parsley

Arrange the eggs, cut side down, in a shallow ovenproof dish. Sprinkle with the corn and shrimps, reserving a few for garnish.

Blend the cornflour with a little of the milk. Heat the remainder, stir into the cornflour mixture, then return to the pan. Heat, stirring, until the sauce thickens. Add the cayenne pepper and salt and pepper to taste, and cook for 2 minutes. Stir in the grated cheese and pour over the eggs.

Cook in a preheated moderate oven, 180°C (350°F), Gas Mark 4, for 15 to 20 minutes. Garnish with paprika, chopped parsley and the reserved shrimps.

Serves 4
Calories per portion: 300 (1256 kJ)

Country Pancakes

PANCAKES:
*125 g (4 oz) plain
    flour*
pinch of salt
1 egg
*300 ml (½ pint)
    skimmed milk*
*15 g (½ oz) lard for
    frying*

FILLING:
*125 g (4 oz)
    mushrooms,
    chopped*
1 onion, sliced
*6 tomatoes, skinned
    and chopped*
*125 g (4 oz) green
    beans*
*1 teaspoon mixed
    herbs*
salt and pepper

TO FINISH:
*100 g (4 oz)
    Lancashire cheese,
    grated*
*parsley sprigs to
    garnish*

Sift the flour and salt into a bowl. Make a well in the centre and add the egg and half the milk. Beat until smooth, then stir in the remaining milk.

Place the filling ingredients, with salt and pepper to taste, in a pan. Bring to the boil, cover and simmer for 10 minutes.

To make the pancakes, lightly grease an 18 cm (7 inch) non-stick frying pan with lard and place over a moderate heat. Pour in enough batter to cover the base. Cook until the underside is lightly browned, then toss or turn the pancake and cook the other side.

Repeat with the remaining batter to make 8 pancakes; stack them on a plate, with a piece of greaseproof paper between each one, over a pan of simmering water to keep hot.

Divide the filling between the pancakes, top with two-thirds of the cheese and fold up. Arrange in an ovenproof dish and sprinkle with the remaining cheese. Place under a preheated hot grill until the cheese is bubbling and golden. Serve immediately, garnished with parsley.

Serves 4
Calories per portion: 300 (1256 kJ)

Crunchy Topped Toast

4 slices low-calorie
 bread
150 g (5 oz)
 Cheddar cheese,
 grated
25 g (1 oz) peanuts,
 chopped
2 small dessert
 apples, peeled,
 cored and grated
1 teaspoon lemon
 juice
1 drop of Tabasco
 sauce
salt and pepper
parsley sprigs to
 garnish

Toast the bread lightly on both sides.
 Mix together the remaining
ingredients, with salt and pepper to
taste, then spread over the toast.
Place under a preheated moderate
grill for about 5 minutes until the
cheese is bubbling and golden. Serve
immediately, garnished with parsley.
Serves 4
Calories per portion: 225 (1942 kJ)

Quick Pizzas

4 slices low-calorie
 bread
15 g (½ oz)
 low-calorie spread
75 g (3 oz) Edam
 cheese, grated
2 tomatoes, sliced
1 teaspoon mixed
 herbs
salt and pepper
50 g (2 oz) lean
 ham, cut into
 strips
TO GARNISH:
tomato wedges
parsley sprigs

Toast the bread lightly on both sides
and cover with the low-calorie
spread.
 Arrange half the cheese on the
toast then top with the tomato slices.
Sprinkle with the mixed herbs and
salt and pepper to taste. Top with the
remaining cheese, then arrange the
ham in a lattice pattern over the top.
 Place under a preheated moderate
grill until the cheese has melted.
Serve immediately, garnished with
parsley and tomato wedges.
Serves 4
Calories per portion: 140 (586 kJ)

Hawaiian Toast

4 slices low-calorie
  bread
150 g (5 oz) natural
  low-fat yogurt
125 g (4 oz)
  Lancashire cheese,
  crumbled
½ green pepper,
  cored, seeded and
  chopped
5 pineapple rings
salt and pepper
parsley sprigs to
  garnish

Toast the bread lightly on both sides.

Mix together the yogurt, cheese, green pepper and 1 chopped pineapple ring. Add salt and pepper to taste. Spread the mixture over the toast and top each with a pineapple ring.

Place under a preheated moderate grill for 4 to 6 minutes or until the cheese begins to bubble and brown.

Serve hot, garnished with a parsley sprig inside each pineapple ring.

Serves 4
Calories per portion: 180 (753 kJ)

Cheese Slaw

250 g (8 oz) white
  cabbage, finely
  shredded
1 celery stick,
  chopped
2 carrots, grated
25 g (1 oz) raisins
1 dessert apple
2 teaspoons lemon
  juice
175 g (6 oz) Gouda
  cheese, coarsely
  grated
150 g (5 oz) natural
  low-fat yogurt
salt and pepper
chopped parsley to
  garnish

Place the cabbage, celery, carrot and
raisins in a large bowl. Grate the
apple and toss in the lemon juice.
Add to the bowl with the cheese and
mix well.

Season the yogurt with salt and
pepper to taste, then stir into the
salad. Pile onto a serving dish and
garnish with chopped parsley.

Serves 4
Calories per portion: 220 (921 kJ)

Farmhouse Grill

4 slices wholemeal
    bread
15 g (½ oz) low-
    calorie spread
2 dessert apples,
    peeled, cored and
    sliced
125 g (4 oz) smoked
    ham sausage,
    sliced
2 tablespoons tomato
    chutney
2 pickled onions,
    finely chopped
125 g (4 oz)
    Cheddar cheese,
    grated
parsley sprigs to
    garnish

Toast the bread lightly on both sides, then cover with the low-calorie spread.

Arrange the apple slices on the toast, then top with the sausage. Spread tomato chutney over the sausage and sprinkle with the pickled onions.

Top with the grated cheese and place under a preheated moderate grill until heated through and the cheese is bubbling and golden. Garnish with parsley.

Serves 4
Calories per portion: 275 (1151 kJ)

53

Cauliflower Cheese Bake

1 medium cauliflower
salt and pepper
150 ml (¼ pint)
 skimmed milk
1 egg, beaten
75 g (3 oz) cheese,
 grated
2 teaspoons paprika
1 tomato, sliced, to
 garnish
250 g (8 oz) lean
 ham (optional)

Remove the outer leaves and stalks from the cauliflower. Wash well and break into florets. Cook in boiling salted water for 5 minutes, then drain.

Beat together the milk, egg, 50 g (2 oz) of the cheese, paprika and salt and pepper to taste.

Place the cauliflower in a lightly greased 1.5 litre (2½ pint) ovenproof dish. Pour the egg mixture over the cauliflower and sprinkle with the remaining cheese. Cook in a preheated moderate oven, 180°C (350°F), Gas Mark 4, for 30 to 40 minutes or until the cheese custard is set. Garnish with tomato slices.

Serve as a snack meal on its own, or with ham for a more substantial meal.

Serves 4
Calories per portion: 135 (565 kJ)
285 (1193 kJ) with ham

Stilton Eggs

4 tablespoons frozen
 mixed vegetables,
 cooked
75 g (3 oz) Stilton
 cheese, crumbled
4 eggs
salt and pepper
2 tablespoons milk
parsley sprigs to
 garnish

Place the mixed vegetables in 4 small, lightly greased ovenproof dishes. Sprinkle 50 g (2 oz) of the cheese over the top.

Break an egg into each dish and sprinkle with salt and pepper. Spoon the milk over the top and sprinkle with the remaining cheese.

Place the dishes in a roasting pan, half-filled with water. Cook in a preheated moderately hot oven, 190°C (375°F), Gas Mark 5, for 15 minutes or until the eggs are set. Garnish with parsley and serve with crispbreads.

Serves 4
Calories per portion: 200 (837 kJ)

Cheese and Ham Wheel

7 g (¼ oz)
  margarine
1 onion, chopped
2 celery sticks,
  chopped
½ green pepper,
  cored, seeded and
  chopped
2 eggs
150 ml (¼ pint)
  skimmed milk
250 g (8 oz) cottage
  cheese
salt and pepper
25 g (1 oz) Cheddar
  cheese, grated
125 g (4 oz) lean
  ham, cut into
  strips
TO GARNISH:
parsley sprigs
tomato slice

Melt the margarine in a pan, add the onion, celery and green pepper and sauté gently until softened. Place in a lightly greased 20 cm (8 inch) flan dish.

Beat together the eggs and milk. Mix in the cottage cheese and season with salt and pepper to taste. Pour into the flan dish.

Sprinkle with the Cheddar cheese and arrange the strips of ham on top, like a wheel. Place in a preheated moderate oven, 180°C (350°F), Gas Mark 4, for 30 minutes or until set and golden brown. Garnish the centre of the wheel with parsley and tomato. Serve hot or cold with salad.
Serves 4
Calories per portion: 220 (921 kJ)

Individual Cheese and Mushroom Soufflés

25 g (1 oz) butter
50 g (2 oz) plain
 flour
300 ml (½ pint)
 skimmed milk
3 eggs, separated
175 g (6 oz)
 mushrooms, finely
 chopped
2 tablespoons
 chopped parsley
75 g (3 oz) Edam
 cheese, finely
 grated
½ teaspoon made
 mustard
salt and pepper

Place the butter, flour and milk in a saucepan and heat, whisking continuously until the sauce thickens. Cook for 2 minutes.

Cool slightly then beat in the egg yolks, mushrooms, parsley, cheese, mustard and salt and pepper to taste.

Whisk the egg whites until stiff and fold into the mixture. Divide between four individual greased soufflé dishes. Place in a preheated moderately hot oven, 190°C (375°F), Gas Mark 5, for 20 to 30 minutes or until well risen and golden brown. Serve immediately.

Serves 4
Calories per portion: 260 (1088 kJ)

Spanish Eggs

7 g (¼ oz)
   margarine
1 onion, finely
   chopped
50 g (2 oz) lean
   bacon, chopped
125 g (4 oz)
   mushrooms, sliced
1 x 397 g (14 oz)
   can tomatoes
salt and pepper
1 teaspoon mixed
   herbs
125 g (4 oz) frozen
   mixed vegetables
8 hard-boiled eggs
chopped parsley to
   garnish

Melt the margarine in a pan, add the onion and bacon and fry until soft. Add the mushrooms, tomatoes with their juice, salt and pepper to taste, herbs and vegetables.

Bring to the boil, cover and simmer for 10 minutes. Add the eggs and cook for 10 to 15 minutes.

Remove the eggs, cut in half and arrange cut side down on a hot serving dish. Pour the sauce over the eggs and garnish with chopped parsley.

Serves 4
Calories per portion: 250 (1047 kJ)

Pasta Jumble

125 g (4 oz) fancy
   pasta shapes
salt and pepper
25 g (1 oz) butter or
   margarine
25 g (1 oz) flour
300 ml (½ pint)
   skimmed milk
½ teaspoon made
   mustard
125 g (4 oz) Double
   Gloucester cheese,
   grated
125 g (4 oz) lean
   ham, chopped
1 green pepper,
   cored, seeded and
   chopped
2 oz (50 g)
   sweetcorn

TO GARNISH:
1 tomato, sliced
parsley sprig

Cook the pasta in plenty of boiling salted water, then rinse and drain.

Melt the butter or margarine in a pan, stir in the flour and cook for 1 minute. Remove from the heat and gradually blend in the milk. Heat, stirring continuously until the sauce thickens. Add salt and pepper to taste, and the mustard; cook for 1 minute.

Stir in the pasta, cheese, ham, green pepper and sweetcorn, mix well and transfer to a shallow ovenproof dish. Place in a preheated moderately hot oven, 190°C (375°F), Gas Mark 5, for 20 minutes.

Garnish with tomato slices and parsley.

Serves 4
Calories per portion: 365 (1530 kJ)

Devilled Scramble and Beans

15 g (½ oz) butter
1 onion, finely
   chopped
1 clove garlic,
   crushed
6 eggs
3 tablespoons milk
1 tablespoon tomato
   ketchup
½ teaspoon made
   mustard
salt and pepper
1 × 446 g (15¾ oz)
   can baked beans
chopped parsley to
   garnish

Melt the butter in a pan, add the onion and garlic and fry until soft.

Beat together the eggs, milk, tomato ketchup, mustard and salt and pepper to taste. Add to the pan and cook over a medium heat, stirring gently, until the mixture is set but still soft.

Heat the baked beans and arrange in a circle on a hot serving dish. Pile the scrambled egg into the centre and sprinkle with chopped parsley. Serve immediately.

Serves 4
Calories per portion: 270 (1130 kJ)

Fruit and Cheese Platter

1 lettuce, washed and
  drained
350 g (12 oz)
  cottage cheese
50 g (2 oz) Edam
  cheese, grated
125 g (4 oz) lean
  ham, diced
salt and pepper
4 large fresh peaches,
  stones removed
  and cut into
  quarters
250 g (8 oz) grapes,
  halved and seeded

Arrange the lettuce on a large
serving platter. Mix together the
cottage cheese, Edam cheese and
ham. Season with salt and pepper to
taste. Mix well and pile into the
centre of the lettuce.

Arrange the peaches and grapes
around the cheese and serve at once.
Serves 4
Calories per portion: 275 (1151 kJ)

61

Cauliflower and Orange Salad

1 medium cauliflower
salt and pepper
2 oranges
1 tablespoon low-
   calorie dressing

Remove the outer leaves and stalk from the cauliflower and break the centre into small florets. Cook in boiling salted water for 5 minutes. Drain and place in a serving bowl.

Peel 1 orange, removing all the pith. Divide into segments and cut each segment in half. Add to the cauliflower. Grate the rind from the remaining orange and sprinkle over the cauliflower and orange segments. Squeeze 2 tablespoons of orange juice and mix with the dressing and salt and pepper to taste. Pour over the salad and chill before serving.

Serves 4
Calories per portion: 35 (147 kJ)

Chinese Vegetables

1 tablespoon oil
1 onion, chopped
1 large carrot, grated
3 chicory heads,
    trimmed and sliced
5 cm (2 inch) piece
    of cucumber,
    chopped
2 tablespoons soy
    sauce
2 teaspoons lemon
    juice
1-2 drops sweetener
salt and pepper
125 g (4 oz) bean
    sprouts, rinsed

Heat the oil in a large shallow pan. Add the onion and carrot and fry quickly for 1 minute. Add the chicory and cucumber and cook for a further 1 minute.

Stir in the soy sauce, lemon juice, sweetener, salt and pepper to taste, and bean sprouts. Cook for 1 to 2 minutes and serve immediately.

Serves 4
Calories per portion: 50 (209 kJ)

Courgettes with Tomatoes

7 g (¼ oz)
    margarine
1 onion, chopped
500 g (1 lb)
    courgettes,
    chopped
6 tomatoes, skinned
    and chopped
salt and pepper

Melt the margarine in a pan, add the onion and fry until soft. Add the courgettes, tomatoes and salt and pepper to taste. Cover and shake the pan. Cook over a low heat until the courgettes are tender, about 30 to 35 minutes. Transfer to a serving dish and serve hot or cold.

Serves 4
Calories per portion: 40 (167 kJ)

Chicory with Lemon Sauce

750 g (1 ½ lb)
  chicory, trimmed
  and washed
salt and pepper
15 g (½ oz)
  low-calorie spread
grated rind and juice
  of 1 small lemon
pinch of grated
  nutmeg
150 ml (¼ pint)
  light stock
2 teaspoons cornflour
1 tablespoon cold
  water
chopped parsley to
  garnish

Blanch the chicory heads in boiling salted water for 3 minutes, then drain. Arrange in a shallow, oven-proof dish and dot with the spread.

Mix together the lemon rind and juice, nutmeg and stock. Season to taste with salt and pepper, then pour over the chicory. Cover with foil and cook in a preheated moderate oven, 160°C (325°F), Gas Mark 3, for 1 hour. Drain off the juices into a small pan. Keep the chicory hot.

Blend the cornflour with the water and stir into the juices. Heat gently, stirring until the sauce thickens, then cook for 1 to 2 minutes. Adjust the seasoning and pour over the chicory. Serve hot, garnished with parsley.
Serves 4
Calories per portion: 55 (230 kJ)

Baked Aubergines

2 aubergines
2 teaspoons salt
15 g (½ oz)
  margarine
1 onion, chopped
1 clove garlic,
  crushed
150 ml (¼ pint)
  stock
3 tomatoes, skinned
  and chopped
1 tablespoon chopped
  chives
1 tablespoon
  sweetcorn
salt and pepper
25 g (1 oz)
  low-calorie
  breadcrumbs
25 g (1 oz) Edam
  cheese, grated

Cut the aubergines in half lengthways, slash the flesh and sprinkle with the salt. Place, cut side down, on a plate and leave for 1 hour. Rinse and drain, then remove and chop the flesh, reserving the skins.

Heat the margarine in a pan, add the onion and fry until soft. Add the aubergine flesh, garlic, 2 tablespoons stock, tomatoes, chives, sweetcorn, salt and pepper to taste; cook until soft. Pile into the aubergine cases.

Place the aubergines in a shallow ovenproof dish. Mix together the breadcrumbs and cheese and sprinkle over the aubergines. Add the remaining stock to the dish, then cover with foil. Place in a preheated moderately hot oven, 190°C (375°F), Gas Mark 5, for 30 minutes. Serve hot with meat or egg dishes.
Serves 4
Calories per portion: 75 (314 kJ)

Leeks with Mustard Sauce

750 g (1½ lb) leeks
salt and pepper
1 tablespoon
  cornflour
300 ml (½ pint)
  skimmed milk
1 teaspoon made
  mustard
1 crispbread, crushed

Trim the leeks, cut in half lengthways and wash thoroughly under cold running water. Cook in boiling salted water for 10 minutes or until tender, then drain. Place in a shallow heatproof dish and keep warm.

Blend the cornflour with a little of the milk. Heat the remaining milk, stir into the cornflour, then return to the pan. Heat, stirring until thickened. Add salt and pepper to taste, and the mustard, then continue cooking for a further 2 minutes. Pour the sauce over the leeks.

Sprinkle the crispbread over the top and place under a preheated hot grill for 1 minute. Serve immediately.
Serves 4
Calories per portion: 95 (398 kJ)

Beans with Tomato Sauce

500 g (1 lb) runner
  beans, sliced
salt and pepper
7 g (¼ oz)
  margarine
1 small onion, finely
  chopped
3 teaspoons tomato
  purée
1-2 drops liquid
  sweetener
150 g (5 oz) natural
  low-fat yogurt

Cook the beans in boiling salted water. Drain and keep hot in a serving dish.

Melt the margarine in a pan, add the onion and fry until soft. Add the tomato purée, salt, pepper and sweetener to taste. Cook for 2 minutes, then stir in the yogurt. Heat gently without boiling then pour over the beans. Serve immediately.
Serves 4
Calories per portion: 60 (251 kJ)

Vegetable Casserole

250 g (8 oz) swede,
   sliced
2 carrots, sliced
1 large onion, sliced
2 celery sticks,
   chopped
salt and pepper
grated nutmeg
1 x 397 g (14 oz)
   can tomatoes
chopped parsley to
   garnish

Lightly grease a 1.75 litre (3 pint) casserole. Arrange the vegetables in the dish in layers, sprinkling each liberally with salt, pepper and nutmeg.

Pour the tomatoes and their juice over the top, cover and cook in a preheated moderate oven, 180°C (350°F), Gas Mark 4, for 1 to 1¼ hours or until the vegetables are tender. Serve hot, garnished with parsley.

Serves 4
Calories per portion: 45 (188 kJ)

Sweet and Sour Red Cabbage

1 medium red
  cabbage, shredded
1 large cooking
  apple, peeled,
  cored and chopped
15 g (½ oz) butter
3 tablespoons wine
  vinegar
1-2 tablespoons
  water
15 g (½ oz) sugar
salt and pepper
1 tablespoon
  redcurrant jelly

Place the cabbage, apple and butter in a saucepan. Cover and cook over a low heat, stirring occasionally, until the butter has melted.

Add the vinegar, water, sugar and salt and pepper to taste. Cover and simmer for 30 to 40 minutes.

Stir in the redcurrant jelly, check the seasoning and cook for 10 minutes. Transfer to a serving dish and serve hot or cold.

Serves 4
Calories per portion: 65 (272 kJ)

Stuffed Tomatoes

4 large tomatoes
25 g (1 oz) Edam
  cheese, diced
125 g (4 oz) cottage
  cheese
15 g (½ oz)
  walnuts, chopped
1 spring onion,
  finely chopped
1 teaspoon chopped
  parsley
salt and pepper
TO GARNISH:
lettuce leaves
watercress
cucumber slices

Cut the top from each tomato and scoop out the inside. Chop the pulp and place in a bowl. Add the Edam and cottage cheese, walnuts, spring onion and parsley. Mix well and season with salt and pepper to taste. Pile the mixture into the tomato shells and replace the lids.

Arrange the lettuce leaves on a serving plate and place the tomatoes in the centre. Garnish with watercress and cucumber slices.

Serves 4
Calories per portion: 85 (356 kJ)

Peppers à Provence

1 tablespoon oil
2 onions, sliced
4 green peppers,
  cored, seeded and
  sliced
1 clove garlic, crushed
1 x 397 g (14 oz)
  can tomatoes
1 teaspoon mixed
  herbs
salt and pepper

Heat the oil in a pan, add the onions and fry until soft. Add the peppers and garlic and cook for 5 minutes.

Stir in the tomatoes and their juice, mixed herbs and salt and pepper to taste. Bring to the boil, then simmer, uncovered, for 15 minutes. Transfer to a serving dish and serve hot or cold.

Serves 4
Calories per portion: 70 (293 kJ)

Chinese Salad

175 g (6 oz) red
cabbage, finely
shredded
few Chinese cabbage
leaves, shredded
125 g (4 oz) bean
sprouts rinsed
2 celery sticks,
chopped
5 cm (2 inch) piece
of cucumber, cut
into strips
DRESSING:
2 tablespoons
low-calorie salad
cream
4 tablespoons natural
low-fat yogurt
1 teaspoon soy sauce
salt and pepper

Place the red cabbage in a bowl and
add the Chinese leaves, bean sprouts,
celery and cucumber.

Mix together the dressing
ingredients, with salt and pepper to
taste, and add to the vegetables. Mix
well and transfer to a serving bowl.
Serves 4
Calories per portion: 35 (147 kJ)

Spanish Coleslaw

250 g (8 oz) white
  cabbage, finely
  shredded
1 small onion, finely
  chopped
½ green pepper,
  cored, seeded and
  chopped
½ red pepper, cored,
  seeded and
  chopped
1 large carrot, grated
50 g (2 oz) grapes,
  halved and seeded
6 tablespoons natural
  low-fat yogurt
1 tablespoon low-
  calorie dressing
salt and pepper
chopped parsley to
  garnish

Place the cabbage in a bowl and add
the onion, green and red peppers,
carrot and grapes.

Mix together the yogurt and
dressing; season with salt and pepper
to taste. Add to the vegetables and
toss thoroughly. Transfer to a
serving bowl and garnish with
parsley.
Serves 4
Calories per portion: 45 (188 kJ)

Spinach and Yogurt

1 kg (2 lb) fresh
  spinach or 500 g
  (1 lb) frozen leaf
  spinach
150 g (5 oz) natural
  low-fat yogurt
1-2 cloves garlic,
  crushed
salt and pepper

Rinse fresh spinach thoroughly and cook in a covered pan, without additional water, until tender. If using frozen spinach, cook according to packet instructions. Drain and cool.

Mix together the yogurt and garlic and stir into the spinach. Add salt and pepper to taste. Transfer to a serving dish.

Serves 4
Calories per portion: 55 (230 kJ)

Curried Mushrooms

150 g (5 oz) natural
  low-fat yogurt
2 tablespoons
  chutney
6 tablespoons
  low-calorie salad
  cream
1 teaspoon curry
  powder
salt and pepper
350 g (12 oz) button
  mushrooms, sliced
chopped parsley to
  garnish

Mix together the yogurt, chutney, salad cream, curry powder and salt and pepper to taste. Add the mushrooms and mix well. Arrange in a serving dish and chill for at least 2 hours before serving. Garnish with the parsley.

Serves 4
Calories per portion: 75 (314 kJ)

Turkish Cucumber Salad

½ cucumber
150 g (5 oz) natural
  low-fat yogurt
salt and pepper
2 tablespoons
  chopped chives

Wash the cucumber and cut into small cubes. Mix with the yogurt, salt and pepper to taste and 1 tablespoon of the chives. Transfer to a serving dish and sprinkle with the remaining chives.

Serves 4
Calories per portion: 30 (126 kJ)

Endive and Grapefruit Salad

1 medium endive
1 grapefruit
3 spring onions,
    chopped
2 tablespoons
    chopped parsley
2 tablespoons low-
    calorie dressing

Wash the endive and break into pieces. Peel the grapefruit, removing all the pith, and divide into segments. Place in a bowl, add the remaining ingredients and toss well.
Serves 4
Calories per portion: 40 (167 kJ)

Mixed Vegetable Salad

½ small cauliflower
125 g (4 oz) carrots,
    sliced
125 g (4 oz) green
    beans
salt and pepper
125 g (4 oz)
    sweetcorn
1 celery stick, chopped
DRESSING:
4 tablespoons natural
    low-fat yogurt
½ teaspoon
    horseradish sauce
½ teaspoon lemon
    juice
TO GARNISH:
chopped parsley

Wash the cauliflower and break into florets. Blanch the cauliflower, carrots and beans in boiling salted water for 5 minutes, then drain and cool.

Mix together the cauliflower, carrots, beans, sweetcorn and celery in a bowl.

Mix the dressing ingredients together and season with salt and pepper to taste. Add to the vegetables, toss and transfer to a serving dish. Garnish with parsley.
Serves 4
Calories per portion: 50 (209 kJ)

Where a recipe requires a low-calorie dressing, try one of the following recipes. Alternatively use a bought variety.

Tomato Dressing

150 ml (¼ pint)
  tomato juice
150 ml (¼ pint)
  vinegar
1 teaspoon grated
  onion
½ teaspoon dried
  mustard
1 teaspoon sugar
½ teaspoon Worcester-
  shire sauce
1 teaspoon chopped
  parsley
salt and pepper

Place all the ingredients, with salt and pepper to taste, in a screw-top jar and shake vigorously until well blended.
Calories per tablespoon: 5 (21 kJ)

Low Calorie French Dressing

1 tablespoon olive oil
6 tablespoons vinegar
3 drops of liquid
  sweetener
½ teaspoon made
  mustard
salt and pepper

Place all the ingredients, with salt and pepper to taste, in a screw-top jar and shake vigorously until well blended.
Calories per tablespoon: 18 (75 kJ)
NOTE: Cider vinegar or wine vinegar should preferably be used.

DESSERTS

Strawberry Mould

250 g (8 oz) cottage cheese, sieved
150 g (5 oz) natural low-fat yogurt
250 g (8 oz) strawberries, puréed
3 teaspoons gelatine
3 tablespoons water
3-4 drops of liquid sweetener
2 egg whites
125 g (4 oz) fresh sliced strawberries, to decorate

Mix together the cottage cheese, yogurt and strawberry purée.

Dissolve the gelatine in the water in a bowl over a pan of gently simmering water. Cool, then fold into the cheese mixture with sweetener to taste.

Whisk the egg whites until stiff and fold into the mixture. Pour into a 20 cm (8 inch) loose bottom flan tin. Chill until set.

Remove from the tin, place on a serving plate and decorate with the strawberries.

Serves 6
Calories per portion: 85 (356 kJ)

Blackberry and Apple Mousse

250 g (8 oz)
  blackberries
250 g (8 oz) apples,
  peeled, cored and
  sliced
6 tablespoons water
few drops of liquid
  sweetener
3 teaspoons gelatine
1 tablespoon lemon
  juice
2 egg whites
TO DECORATE:
75 ml (2½ fl oz)
  whipping cream,
  whipped
  (optional)
few blackberries

Wash the blackberries and place in a pan with the apples and 2 tablespoons of the water. Cook gently until the fruit is soft, then add sweetener to taste. Leave to cool, then pass through a sieve to make a purée and remove the pips.

Dissolve the gelatine in the remaining water, in a bowl placed over a pan of gently simmering water. Stir in the lemon juice and leave to cool. Add the gelatine to the fruit and blend thoroughly.

Whisk the egg whites until stiff and fold into the mixture. Pour into 4 serving dishes and leave until set.

Decorate with the whipped cream, if using, and blackberries.

Serves 4
Calories per portion: 135 (565 kJ)
50 (209 kJ) without cream

*Strawberry mould;
Cinnamon plums (page
78); Blackberry and apple
mousse.*

Cinnamon Plums

250 g (8 oz) dessert
plums
1 teaspoon ground
cinnamon
2 egg yolks
300 g (10 oz)
natural low-fat
yogurt
½ teaspoon vanilla
essence
2 drops of liquid
sweetener
25 g (1 oz)
cornflakes, crushed

Cut the plums in half, discard the stones and place in a 600 ml (1 pint) ovenproof dish or 4 individual dishes. Sprinkle the plums with ½ teaspoon cinnamon.

Beat the egg yolks with the yogurt, vanilla essence and sweetener and pour over the plums.

Place in a roasting pan and add water to come halfway up the dish(es). Cook in a preheated moderate oven, 180°C (350°F), Gas Mark 4, for 30 minutes or until set.

Mix the cornflakes with the remaining cinnamon and sprinkle over the custard. Serve hot or cold.

Serves 4
Calories per portion: 90 (377 kJ)
Illustrated on page 76.

Strawberry Cheesecake

BASE:
25 g (1 oz) butter
5 low-calorie
digestive biscuits,
crushed
FILLING:
150 ml (¼ pint)
water
½ packet lime jelly
1 tablespoon lemon
juice
grated rind of 1
lemon
250 g (8 oz) cottage
cheese, sieved
TOPPING:
1½ teaspoons
arrowroot
2 tablespoons lemon
juice
6 tablespoons water
250 g (8 oz)
strawberries,
washed and hulled

Melt the butter and mix with the biscuit crumbs. Press into the base of a lightly greased 18 cm (7 inch) flan ring on a serving plate, or into a flan dish. Leave until firm.

To make the filling: heat the water in a pan and add the jelly. Stir until dissolved, then leave to cool. Add the lemon juice, rind and cottage cheese. Mix well and pour over the biscuit base. Chill in the refrigerator until set. Remove the ring, if used.

To make the topping: blend the arrowroot with the lemon juice in a small pan, then stir in the water. Heat, stirring, until the mixture thickens and clears. Leave to cool a little.

Decorate the cheesecake with the strawberries and spoon the glaze over the top. Chill before serving.

Serves 6
Calories per portion: 140 (586 kJ)

Somerset Pears

200 ml (⅓ pint) dry
  cider
2 teaspoons lemon
  juice
½ teaspoon ground
  cinnamon
pinch of grated
  nutmeg
grated rind of 1
  orange
4 dessert pears
few drops of liquid
  sweetener

Place the cider, lemon juice,
cinnamon, nutmeg and orange rind
in a pan. Bring to the boil, cover and
simmer for 5 minutes.

Peel the pears, cut in half and
remove the core. Place in the liquid
and poach for 20 to 30 minutes or
until soft. Add sweetener to taste.

Lift the pears into a serving dish
and pour the liquid over. Serve hot
or cold with natural low-fat yogurt
or a little single cream.

Serves 4
Calories per portion: 60 (251 kJ)

Pineapple Sorbet

1 x 382 g (13½ oz)
  can crushed
  pineapple
50 g (2 oz) caster
  sugar
1 tablespoon lemon
  juice
300 g (10 oz)
  natural low-fat
  yogurt

Drain the pineapple and pour the
juice into a pan. Add the sugar and
lemon juice and heat until dissolved.
Leave to cool then stir in the yogurt.

Pour into a shallow rigid container
and freeze until the mixture is
mushy. Remove from the freezer and
stir in the crushed pineapple. Return
to a rigid container, cover and freeze
until solid.

Transfer to the refrigerator about 1
hour before required. Spoon into
sundae dishes to serve.

Serves 6
Calories per portion: 110 (460 kJ)

Orange Honey Fluff

25 g (1 oz) honey
grated rind and juice
  of 1 orange
2 teaspoons lemon
  juice
300 g (10 oz)
  natural low-fat
  yogurt
2 egg whites
few strips of orange
  rind to decorate

Blend the honey with the orange and
lemon juice. Stir in the grated orange
rind and yogurt.

Whisk the egg whites until stiff
and fold into the mixture. Spoon
into 4 sundae dishes and decorate
with the orange rind. Serve chilled.

Serves 4
Calories per portion: 75 (314 kJ)
NOTE: Do not stand for more than 1
hour or the mixture will separate.

Apple and Pear Crumble

250 g (8 oz) apples,
  peeled, cored and
  sliced
250 g (8 oz) pears,
  peeled, cored and
  sliced
grated rind of 1
  lemon
½ teaspoon ground
  cinnamon
1 tablespoon water
few drops of liquid
  sweetener
TOPPING:
50 g (2 oz)
  Swiss-style muesli
25 g (1 oz) porridge
  oats
25 g (1 oz)
  cornflakes, crushed

Place the apples and pears in a pan with the lemon rind, cinnamon and water. Cook gently until the fruit is soft, but not pulpy. Add sweetener to taste and spoon into a 1.2 litre (2 pint) ovenproof dish.

Mix together the muesli, porridge oats and cornflakes and pile on top of the fruit. Cook in a preheated moderately hot oven, 190°C (375°F), Gas Mark 5, for 15 minutes or until the topping is crisp. Serve hot.
Serves 4
Calories per portion: 145 (607 kJ)

Blackcurrant Fool

1 tablespoon custard
   powder
300 ml (½ pint)
   skimmed milk
few drops of liquid
   sweetener
300 g (10 oz)
   blackcurrants
1 tablespoon water
150 g (5 oz) natural
   low-fat yogurt
few blackcurrants
   to decorate

Blend the custard powder with a
little of the milk. Heat the remaining
milk and stir into the custard
mixture, then return to the pan.
Heat, stirring continuously until the
custard thickens. Cook for 1 minute.
Add sweetener to taste and leave to
cool.

Trim and wash the blackcurrants,
then place in a pan with the water.
Cook gently until the fruit is soft.
Add sweetener to taste and leave to
cool. Place the fruit in an electric
blender or pass through a sieve to
make a purée.

Add the fruit purée and yogurt to
the custard and whisk until well
blended. Spoon into 4 individual
serving dishes and decorate with
blackcurrants. Chill before serving.

Serves 4
Calories per portion: 80 (335 kJ)

Apricot and Banana Compote

125 g (4 oz) dried
   apricots
2 bananas
2 teaspoons lemon
   juice
25 g (1 oz) raisins
150 g (5 oz) natural
   low-fat yogurt
few drops of liquid
   sweetener
   (optional)
grated nutmeg

Wash the apricots, place in a bowl
and cover with cold water. Leave to
soak overnight.

Slice the bananas and toss in the
lemon juice. Place the apricots in a
bowl with a little of the soaking
liquid. Add the bananas and raisins,
then divide the fruit between 4 glass
serving dishes.

Sweeten the yogurt if preferred,
spoon over the fruit and sprinkle
with grated nutmeg. Chill before
serving.

Serves 4
Calories per portion: 130 (544 kJ)

Gooseberry Meringue

500 g (1 lb)
   gooseberries
1 tablespoon water
few drops of liquid
   sweetener
2 egg whites
75 g (3 oz) caster
   sugar

Top and tail the gooseberries and wash well. Place in a pan with the water. Cook gently until the fruit is soft, then add sweetener to taste. Spoon into a 900 ml (1½ pint) ovenproof dish.

Whisk the egg whites until stiff, then whisk in half the sugar. Fold in the remaining sugar with a metal spoon and pile or pipe the meringue over the gooseberries. Place in a preheated moderate oven, 180°C (350°F), Gas Mark 4, for 15 minutes or until the meringue is just turning brown. Serve hot or cold.

Serves 4
Calories per portion: 130 (544 kJ)

Mincemeat Baked Apples

4 × 150 g (5 oz)
  cooking apples
50 g (2 oz)
  mincemeat
150 ml (¼ pint)
  apple juice
4 tablespoons single
  cream (optional)

Remove the core from the apples and
score the skin around the middle. Fill
the centre with the mincemeat.

Place in a shallow ovenproof dish
and pour the apple juice over. Bake
in a preheated moderately hot oven,
190°C (375°F), Gas Mark 5, for 30
minutes or until the apples are soft.
Serve with the cream, if using.

Serves 4
Calories per portion: 135 (565 kJ)
105 (439 kJ) without cream

Rhubarb and Orange Crunch

500 g (1 lb) rhubarb,
  chopped
grated rind and juice
  of 1 orange
few drops of liquid
  sweetener
150 g (5 oz)
  mandarin low-fat
  yogurt
4 low-calorie
  digestive biscuits,
  crushed
¼ teaspoon mixed
  spice
2 slices orange to
  decorate

Place the rhubarb in a pan with the orange rind and juice. Stew until the fruit is soft, then add sweetener to taste. Leave to cool.

Place the fruit in an electric blender or pass through a sieve to make a purée. Stir in the yogurt and spoon the mixture into 4 glass serving dishes.

Mix the biscuits with the mixed spice and spoon over the fruit. Chill in the refrigerator until required.

Cut the orange slices into quarters and use 2 to decorate each crunch.

Serves 4
Calories per portion: 80 (335 kJ)

Raspberry and Peach Pancakes

PANCAKES:
125 g (4 oz) plain
  flour
pinch of salt
1 egg
300 ml (½ pint)
  skimmed milk
15 g (½ oz) lard for
  frying
FILLING:
4 peaches, stoned and
  sliced
175 g (6 oz)
  raspberries
1 tablespoon water
few drops of liquid
  sweetener
TO DECORATE:
sifted icing sugar

Sift the flour and salt into a bowl. Make a well in the centre and add the egg and half the milk. Beat until smooth, then stir in the remaining milk.

Lightly grease an 18 cm (7 inch) non-stick frying pan with the lard and place over moderate heat. Pour in enough batter to cover the base of the pan. Cook until the underside is browned, then toss or turn the pancake and cook the other side.

Repeat with the remaining batter to make 8 pancakes; stack them on a plate, with a piece of greaseproof paper between each one, over a pan of simmering water to keep hot.

Place the peaches in a pan with the raspberries and water. Cook gently until the peaches are soft. Add sweetener to taste. Divide the filling between the pancakes and roll or fold. Arrange on a warm serving dish and sprinkle with icing sugar.

Serves 4
Calories per portion: 200 (837 kJ)

Orange and Pineapple Jelly

150 ml (¼ pint)
    water
1 packet orange jelly
200 ml (⅓ pint)
    pineapple juice
150 g (5 oz) natural
    low-fat yogurt
orange twists to
    decorate

Heat the water in a pan and add the jelly. Stir until dissolved, then add the pineapple juice. Pour into a bowl and place in the refrigerator until just beginning to set.

Whisk in the yogurt until well blended, then pour into 4 glass serving dishes. Leave until set, then decorate with orange twists.

Serves 4
Calories per portion: 150 (628 kJ)

Sunset Fruit Salad

1 Ogen melon
250 g (8 oz) grapes
250 g (8 oz)
    strawberries
grated rind and juice
    of 1 orange
1 tablespoon sherry
1 tablespoon caster
    sugar
½ teaspoon ground
    ginger
150 g (5 oz) natural
    low-fat yogurt
4 pieces preserved
    ginger to decorate

Peel the melon and cut into cubes. Cut the grapes in half and remove the pips. Wash and hull the strawberries and cut into slices. Place all the fruit in a bowl.

Mix together the orange rind, juice, sherry, sugar and ground ginger. Pour over the fruit and leave to soak for several hours, stirring occasionally.

Spoon the fruit into glass serving dishes, top with the yogurt and decorate with preserved ginger.

Serves 4
Calories per portion: 130 (544 kJ)

Raspberry Gâteau

SPONGE BASE:
2 eggs
50 g (2 oz) caster
    sugar
50 g (2 oz) plain
    flour, sifted
1 tablespoon dry
    sherry
TOPPING:
142 ml (5 fl oz)
    fresh sour cream
150 g (5 oz)
    raspberry low-fat
    yogurt
250 g (8 oz)
    raspberries
TO DECORATE:
125 g (4 oz)
    raspberries
25 g (1 oz) caster
    sugar

Grease and line a 20 cm (8 inch) sandwich tin with greased, greaseproof paper.

Put the eggs and sugar in a bowl, place over a pan of hot water and whisk until the mixture is pale in colour and thick enough to leave a trail with the whisk. Remove the bowl from the pan and continue whisking until the mixture is cool.

Quickly fold in the flour with a metal spoon. Pour into the prepared tin and bake in a preheated moderately hot oven, 190°C (375°F), Gas Mark 5, for 15 to 20 minutes until the sponge springs back when pressed lightly.

Leave in the tin for 5 minutes then cool on a wire rack. Place the sponge on a serving plate, prick all over and sprinkle with the sherry.

For the topping: mix together the cream and yogurt. Fold in the raspberries and pile the mixture onto the sponge. Decorate with raspberries and sprinkle with caster sugar. Chill before serving.

Serves 6
Calories per portion: 200 (837 kJ)

Blackcurrant Brûlée

500 g (1 lb)
    blackcurrants
1 tablespoon water
few drops of liquid
    sweetener
142 ml (5 fl oz)
    fresh sour cream
25 g (1 oz) brown
    sugar
15 g (½ oz) flaked
    almonds

Remove the stalks from the blackcurrants and wash well. Place in a pan with the water and cook gently until soft. Add sweetener to taste.

Divide the fruit between 4 heatproof dishes, then place in the refrigerator to chill thoroughly.

Top with the cream and sprinkle with the sugar and almonds. Place under a preheated moderate grill until the sugar has melted and the almonds are brown. Serve immediately.

Serves 4
Calories per portion: (155 (649 kJ)

Food Energy Values

Unless otherwise stated, the calorie (kJ) values below apply to a fresh, raw quantity of 25 g (slightly less than 1 oz, because 1 oz = 28.3 g). These values refer to the edible portion, i.e. without bone, skin, etc.

Food	Cal.	kJ
Almond, shelled	145	608
Apple (1 medium)	50	209
Apricot, fresh	5	21
Apricot, dried	45	188
Aubergine	5	21
Bacon, lean	115	481
Banana (1 medium)	70	293
Bean sprout	neg	neg
Beans, baked	20	84
Beans, broad	15	63
Beans, runner	neg	neg
Beef, lean rump steak	35	147
Beef, lean stewing steak	45	188
Beer (600 ml/1 pint)	145	608
Blackberry	10	42
Blackcurrant	10	42
Bread, brown or white	60	251
Bread, wholemeal	55	230
Broccoli	5	21
Brussels sprout	5	21
Butter	190	795
Cabbage	5	21
Carrot	5	21
Cauliflower	5	21
Celery	neg	neg
Cheese, Cheddar	105	460
Cheese, Cottage (low-fat)	25	105
Cheese, Edam	80	335
Cheese, Gloucester	95	398
Cheese, Gouda	85	356
Cheese, Leicester	95	398
Cheese, Parmesan	105	460
Cheese, Stilton	85	356
Chicken	35	147
Chicory	5	21

Food	Cal.	kJ
Cider, dry (600 ml/1 pint)	180	793
Cod	20	84
Cornflour	90	377
Corn oil	230	963
Courgette	5	21
Cream, double	115	481
Cream, fresh sour	50	209
Crispbread, Sainsbury's (1 slice)	30	126
Cucumber	5	21
Currant	65	272
Egg (1 size 1)	85	356
Egg (1 size 3)	70	293
Endive	5	21
Flour, white	90	377
Flour, wholewheat	80	356
Frankfurter, Sainsbury's	65	272
Garlic, 1 clove	neg	neg
Gooseberry, dessert	10	42
Grape	15	63
Grapefruit	5	21
Grapefruit juice, fresh or canned unsweetened	10	42
Haddock	20	84
Ham, boiled, lean	55	230
Herring (1 whole)	160	670
Herring, soused (1 rollmop)	75	314
Honey	80	335
Horseradish sauce (1 tablespoon)	15	63
Jelly, made	15	63

Food	Cal.	kJ	Food	Cal.	kJ
Kidney	25	105	Prawn, shelled	30	126
Kipper	55	230			
			Raisin	65	272
Lamb, lean	65	272	Raspberry	5	21
Leek	5	21	Redcurrant	5	21
Lemon	5	21	Rhubarb	neg	neg
Lettuce	5	21	Rice	90	377
Liver	40	167			
			Salmon	55	230
			Salmon, canned	40	167
Mackerel	30	126	Sardine, canned	55	230
Mandarins, canned	15	63	Sausage, beef	60	251
Margarine	190	795	Sausage, pork	70	293
Mayonnaise, low-calorie	45	188	Sherry, dry (1 measure)	55	230
Melon	5	21	Shrimp, shelled	35	147
Milk, pasteurized (600 ml/1 pint)	380	1591	Spinach	5	21
			Stock cube	30	126
Milk, skimmed (600 ml/1 pint)	190	795	Strawberry	5	21
Milk, skimmed, powdered	95	398	Sugar	100	418
Milk, evaporated, canned	40	167	Sultana	65	272
			Swede	5	21
Muesli, Sainsbury's	100	418	Sweetcorn, canned	20	84
Mushroom	5	21	Sweetcorn, frozen	25	105
Onion	5	21	Tomato	5	21
Orange	10	42	Tomato, canned	5	21
Orange juice, fresh or canned unsweetened	10	42	Tomato, ketchup	25	105
			Tomato, purée	20	84
			Tomato soup, canned	30	126
Parsnip	15	63	Tuna, canned	70	293
Pasta	95	398	Turkey	35	147
Peach	10	42			
Peanuts, salted	145	608	Veal, lean	30	126
Pear	10	42	Vermouth, dry (1 measure)	55	230
Pear, canned	20	84			
Peas	20	84	Walnut, shelled	135	565
Pepper, red or green	5	21	Watercress	5	21
Pineapple	15	63	Wine, dry (150 ml/ ¼ pint)	90	377
Pineapple, canned	20	84			
Plaice	25	105			
Plum	10	42	Yeast extract	neg	neg
Pork, lean	65	272	Yogurt, natural low-fat	15	63
Potato	25	105	Yogurt, flavoured	25	105

Acknowledgments

Photography by Fred Mancini
Food prepared by Heather Lambert
Designed by Astrid Publishing Consultants Ltd

INDEX